Tony Owens' wonderful undulating poems flow with the ease and power of the river they evoke. The are awash with the theology of place, rooted yet spreading heavenwards. They are songs of the exiled heart. —Joseph Pearce, author of *Tolkien: Man and Myth, The Quest for Shakespeare, Solzhenitsyn: A Soul in Exile, Through Shakespeare's Eyes*

In 1973, the Keowee Valley in northwest South Carolina was submerged by a man-made dam, but in this superb collection of poems Tony Owens has resurrected the valley and allowed it, though erased physically, not to be erased in our memory. Each poem has the precision and vividness to stand alone, but they interweave to create a deeply moving narrative of a lost world.
—Ron Rash, author of *Eureka Mill, Serena, One Foot in Eden, The Cove*

Keowee River Songs

Keowee River Songs

Tony Owens

REDHAWK
PUBLICATIONS

Copyright © 2022 Tony J. Owens

Towens1296@gmail.com

All rights reserved. This book or parts thereof may not be reproduced in any form, stored in any retrieval system, or transmitted in any form by any means—electronic, mechanical, photocopy, recording, or otherwise—without prior written permission of the publisher, except as provided by United States of America copyright law. For permission requests, write to the publisher, at «Attention: Permissions Coordinator,» at the address below.

Redhawk Publications

The Catawba Valley Community College Press

2550 US Hwy 70 SE

Hickory, NC 28602

ISBN: 978-1-952485-61-9

Library of Congress Number: 2022932654

Page 6 photo courtesy of Tim Simpson.

Cover By glassblower - https://www.flickr.com/photos/glassblower/3696564290/, CC BY 2.0, https://commons.wikimedia.org/w/index.php?curid=17277373

Back cover photograph courtesy of Robert Markway

There is a river, the streams whereof shall make glad the city of God.
Psalm 46:4

To Leslie, *l'amor che move il sole e l'altre stele*

Keowee River, c. 1965

Contents

Preface	9
The Bride	11
Currents	12
Bartram at the River – Waiting for Light	13
Bartram at the River – Relics	15
Bartram at the River – Plants	16
Michaux Remembers Three Ruined Towns on the River	17
Rain	18
Sunday School	19
Spring Lizards	21
Telephone Fishing	22
Long Man	23
Twice Buried	24
Mile Creek	25
McKinney's Chapel	26
Requiem for a River	27
Was a River	30
Wait	31
The Song	32
Acknowledgments	34
About the Author	35

Keowee River Songs

Preface

The Keowee River arose several hundred million years ago in the southern Appalachian mountains of the Carolinas. The river was formed from the confluence of the Whitewater (Jocassee), Thompson, Toxaway and Horsepasture Rivers and formed a major tributary of the Savannah River system. The upper river alternated between gentle rapids and deep pools and flowed through a valley of stunning natural beauty and abundant flora and wildlife.

The Cherokee named the river Kuwahi, "place of the mulberry groves," and established numerous towns on its South Carolina banks, including the largest of the Lower Towns, called Keowee. Fur traders moved into the river valley in the early 18th century. In 1754 Fort Prince George was built on the eastern bank of the river to protect the traders and the Cherokee from Creek war parties.

By 1760 smallpox, famine and rising tensions between traders, soldiers, and the Cherokee led to hostilities. Two punitive military expeditions were sent into the valley. All the towns on the river were burned, many of the Cherokee were killed, and most of the remainder retreated to the higher mountains of North Carolina and Tennessee.

White farmers began to enter the valley in the 1770s and 80s. During this period the celebrated botanists William Bartram and Andre Michaux followed the river and discovered a wealth of new plant species, including the rare Oconee Bell. Thousands of specimens were shipped to European gardens, and Bartram's fulsome descriptions of Jocassee valley influenced the poets of the English Romantic movement.

For the next two centuries the Keowee River was host to small farms, hunters, loggers, moonshiners, summer camps and vacation cabins. In the 1960's a subsidiary of Duke Power Company began purchasing the land along the river. In 1965 Duke Power and the state of South Carolina announced plans to construct a nuclear power complex in the Keowee river valley, and the remaining landowners were forced to sell. Vast amounts of timber, including many 200-year-old hardwoods, were harvested as the valley was stripped. In 1973 an earth and rock dam was completed and the upper Keowee river valley was flooded to form what is now Lake Jocassee.

In 1973 the National Wild and Scenic Rivers System was created by Congress to "preserve rivers with outstanding natural, cultural, and recreational values in a free-flowing condition for the enjoyment of present and future generations."

The Bride

Et omnes ad quos pervenit aqua ista, salvi facti sunt. Vidi Aquam

She walks into the river wearing white,
Steps through rocks and clay and finds
Her place, the water now above her thighs,
The current quiet behind the rocks piled

High to make a pool where the man, waist-deep,
waits; she hears above the water's deep chord
the songs of her companions on the shore.
The river takes her and she sinks beneath

The flow. Small trout arise, songbirds awake,
A breeze enlivens the attendant trees;
Gold leaves release and leap into the stream.
 She rises into the sun's bright array.

The dancing of the water still abides;
The river moves in concert with the bride.

Currents

For everything shall live where the river flows. Ezekiel 47:9

Redtails rising in a sky unstained,
Silent on the thermals above the river.
You in the rapids' clamor and clang,
the water red and fitful after rain.

Safe in the channel where the light resides,
Where the live water shivers in the wind;
One with the river's meter and pulse,
Advancing at the current's command.

Skirting the dark depths of old drownings,
Wary of the dim and tangled shore
Where moccasins reside and striders
Glide on the water without sound.

Secure in the flow you come in time
To the place where a new stream arrives;
You witness a union where two become one,
You see a new river arise.

And nimble and wet in the ferment and flood,
You ride that river home.

Tony Owens

Bartram at the River – Waiting for Light

William Bartram (1739-1823), America's first great naturalist, was born in Pennsylvania of a Quaker family. He traveled through the Keowee River valley in 1775, recording and collecting plants. His paternal grandfather was killed in the Tuscarora Indian uprising at coastal North Carolina.

In the black nights, new moon, stars cloud-hidden,

I dream of father's garden at the wide river,

Plants like files on parade, the proper Latin labels,

Quiet as the black-clad Friends on the bench

In the Meeting House, patient for illumination.

And beside this loud and restive river I stir

In the night's reverberation, the insects' pulse and fall,

And listen above the water's agitation for wild boar

rooting logs, for the black cat the hunters called "pa'nter"

That cries in the night like a lost child.

Alone in a wild country I left the fort now trading post

and climbed to higher ground, where the tribes

Had fled, gone over the mountains after the burning

of the towns, wary among the ruined mounds

and shallow graves, war residue in the menacing shade.

Grandfather! Namesake, dead before my birth
Beside a black and torpid river on a fearful cape,
Tuscarora tomahawks and the flashing knife,
The light you awaited coming fitful and cruel
In the fire of that coruscating dawn.

And beside this quick and restless river, I wait
For graying over the Eastern hills, when the mist
Will rise and the water streak silver
And the young deer come without sound to drink
And the light break upon the bright shards of the morning.

Bartram at the River – Relics

Alone, I followed the river's grave lament
Into a country of the dispossessed.
Among burnt crops and raw dirt mounds,
I fingered charred bones and specimens.

Riding higher I heard the river's voice
Increase; white water splintered over stones
Worn luminous in the bright disquiet;
A rainbow quavered in the shattering spray.

In an upper valley I found plowed fields
and young blades rising and a remnant left
behind, where late sun broke through clouds
and fell like seed into furrowed ground.

And picking up cuttings I came to see
How the torn bark of the red oak resides
In the green acorn, how the light within the river
rises only in the breaking of the flow.

Bartram at the River – Plants
I loved plants as men love women,
The orange azalea radiant in the sun,
Ardent as the glow on the copper limbs
Of the girls surprised at the river,
Who brought us wild strawberries,
And peaches that burst as we ate them.
    . . . . .Vegetable beings are endued with sensible faculties or attributes.

I saw the riverbank arrayed like a bride,
The siren-scented jasmine with serpentine
Vine, yellow flowers profligate and sweet,
Bell-like blossoms cloistered in deep shade,
 Forever wet and moving in the spray
of white water dropping into darkness.
    . . . . .Vegetables have the power of moving and exercising their members.

I knew the wide magnolia, pungent and adorned,
The sweetgum stars, the oaks regnant and serene
In the windless mornings but frantic and fierce
In the storms that smoked through the valley
And left seared trees dripping in spent silence.
I saw high leaves honey-colored in the late light
That lingered and tempered the rain-scoured sky.

  And I saw, beneath the world's attire,
  The purity and potency of fire.

Michaux Remembers Three Ruined Towns on the River

Andre Michaux (1746-1802), born on a farm at Versailles, was sent to Spain and Persia as Royal Botanist. He followed the Keowee River to its headwaters in 1787, collecting floral specimens for shipment to France.

Keowee, mulberry place, trees heavy with the blood-red fruit,

Smilax spines and the rifled graves of dead chiefs.

    Was not Versailles and the garden geometry of the doomed King.

Was wasted fields and wild jasmine and the fort across the wide river.

Kulsetyi, place of the honey locust, sweet fierce trees thorn-armored

And wasp-loud in the noon glare, rotting peaches in the copperhead shade.

    Was not La Roca above the abyss, wild orchids on the pilgrims' way.

Was purple laurel trailing in the river and the stone weirs abandoned.

Toxaway, place of thunder, where the white torrent plunged and shattered

On black boulders, where broken oaks glistened in the bright tumult.

    Was not Tehran, the Shah cured of fever and salah *in the scented air.*

Was the white bell flower bending in the spray and wolves wailing in the wet nights.

Was always the light moving on the water and the quick wind in the trees,

Was *Jocassee*, the two streams meeting and the river made new.

Rain

The dogs wouldn't come out in the rain,
Even for Porter who had bred and raised them,
And Price said *'cause they got more sense*
than to leave a warm certainty for a cold
Expectation, and I thought too that a dog
knows, if a man doesn't, that February
down here with a west wind is still winter.
So Porter said *let's ride up to Jocassee,*
And driving through the needles of the rain
Trying to be sleet, we left the mill town,
The closed stores and empty churches,
Passed the flooded unplanted bottoms
And climbed the steep and glassy road,
Windows fogging. Price said *you better be glad*
you can't see what we are just missing.
Then over the rise and into the drenched valley
 We heard through pines and black branches
The crash and chaos of the brown river.
Price said *pull over, I've got to water some bushes,*
and stamping and shaking on the icy bank
I said *hurry up man that water looks cold.*
And in the musty car I thought of the Cherokee,
Desperate with the old remedy for the smallpox
caught from the traders, running from the sweat lodge
to the bitter river to wash away the contagion and stain,
and dying in the rain.

Sunday School

He used to say *let's go up to the river*
And gig frogs. Sweat-stained shirt half covering
A belly like a cotton bale, face pocked with scars
And drink. My first job, Sunday morning cleanup,
Perfect church attendance pin now an air hose
To blow the cotton dust from frames and floors.

He lived near the mill in a company house,
Arrived foul from the night with a six-pack,
Drank the first two, squalid on the mill steps,
And with a belch and a *goddamnit* headed upstairs
Where the big frames lay dormant and dirty
Like penitents at a river or a font.

As the beer mixed with the dust he would get
Mean or playful, you couldn't tell the difference,
But you wouldn't let him catch you with his hose
And you on a ladder or bent over sweeping out a frame.
We would finish at noon, lint-laden, and leave the mill
As the Sunday-clean were coming out of church.

Keowee River Songs

Nights on the river he would blind frogs with a light
And spear them with a gig like the drawing
Of the devil's trident in my Sunday School book,
The frogs skewered and displayed like saints'
Heads, legs severed, bodies tossed into the water,
Vain offerings to indifferent gods.

Spring Lizards

You could use stones and clay to dam
One of the small creeks to make a pond
For the salamanders, God's slimy and prodigal
Palette – bright orange like a sunset
After rain, red and black with bright circles.
We called them spring lizards and heard they
Could live in fire and if they lost a limb
it would grow back, but we didn't believe that
until we found one with a healthy nub
Where a leg used to be.

In the morning the lizards and the dam
Were gone; the creek running cold and clear
To the spring where the dipper was hung;
The only colors left were pebbles that flashed
Red and orange in the sunlit water but dulled
like dying trout when you picked them up to keep.

Years later I dreamed the big dam had burst,
Earthquake or age, and the buried river was awake
And racing through the seared and blasted valley,
Years of lake trash were washing away like sins;
On both banks new shoots sprouted into laurel
And jasmine; rainbows returned to the silver rapids,
And the sound of the river was laughter and applause.

Telephone Fishing

If you stood in the rapids and turned over
Smooth rocks of the right size you could pick
Off hellgrammites clinging to the undersides.
They were fine catfish bait but were armored
Like predators and you had to be wary of the jaws.

Or you could wire a magneto from an old phone,
And standing on a rock drop the two leads
Into the river, and turning the crank
You could put a hundred volts into the water
And the fish would float up like raptured souls,
White bellies rising from the green depths
Like shrouded saints in old frescoes.

I once saw two men fishing with a phone,
One turned the crank the other slipped
On mossy rocks and fell into the current.
The beer he had been drinking spiked the water
And caressed him like a hairshirt and he bounced
like the flat stones you could skip over the water
three or four times before they sank and were gone.

Long Man

Gunahita asgaya – long man, head in the mountains and feet in the sea

Tall corn tousling in due time,
New peaches heavy on the bough,
The jay's quick flash, the wood thrush chime,
The river never costive or foul.

At first dawn the warriors arrive,
When sun fires the water to gold,
Wading into light, the river alive
and waiting, the ablution pure and cold.

And this will endure, the treaties declared,
As long as the river flows, as long as light flares
On live water, as long as *long man*
Rolls through a green and vestal land.

Twice Buried

For the trumpet shall sound, and the dead shall be raised. 1 Cor 15:52

They startle divers in the blackest depths,
Caught unawares, furtive in the lamp's green light,
At the bottom where the monuments reside.

Under silt and boat debris, long bereft
Of mourners, flowers, and wreaths.
These are the twice buried, sextons of the silent stream.

Ever anxious for the distant call,
Aching to rise through water and earth,
Desperate for another birth.

Mile Creek

Montgomery's Raid - 1760
The Colonel had silenced the pipes
For the night march by the river.
A dog barking in the watery dawn
Told us of the town; fires still smoldered
as we charged, yelling; in a surfeit
of mercy we spared the women
and the children; some took scalps
for the bounty. Barely a town, the rough
Huts by the creek went up like kindling
As the sun burned away the cold
And turned the river from red to gold.

The Bridge - 1960
Grandfather would walk us to the creek,
The only time we saw him without a shirt,
His back mill-muscled, quilted and pale
As frayed sheets drying. Daring each other
We jumped from the splintered bridge
Into shallow water and mud, not far,
Until a cousin landed on broken glass
And the blood rose like a scream
And washed away as the water cleared.
Years later we found grandfather at the bridge
Looking for the home he couldn't find,
Staring at the creek as the light disappeared.

McKinney's Chapel

The guard at the gatehouse will let you in
Without a pass, but only as far as the chapel
On the old circuit riders' path, now restored,
A landmark on the way to the new lake
And golf course and the homes of the just arrived.

I walked into the chapel once and heard
I think that part is supposed to be fortè,
A decorous choir, their faces burnished and tight
As the sun sheen on the new cars parked outside
By the scarred and angled tombstones.

McKinney's Ford, where soldiers crossed to burn
The towns and claimed the bounty and the land,
Cleared the red hills, mule-plowed the bottoms
And raised the corn and chickens and children
In the wet winters and storm-seared summers,

Who raised the walls resonant of births and deaths,
When the chapel rang with shaped-noted songs
And sermons, when hard men *got right* at the altar,
When calloused feet were bared and caressed,
And the singing was bold with water and the blood.

Requiem for a River

There's beauty in that silver singing river. Bob Dylan

If you come this way, the old way,
You will pass on the right the white
Baptist church, sentinel in hot light,
Worn stones leaning in the red clay.

When the road turns and begins to sink,
You stop the car; where pavement slides
Under dark water you hear wide
Waves lapping like laughter. You think:

This does not belong here, this slow,
Labored rise and fall, this apostate
Communion of water and road. You wade
Into the shallows. The late sun glows

And flashes and suddenly you're back
As a boy when the road followed the river
And you could smell it before you ever
Saw it through privet and the red sumac.

And you could hear it moving like a thing alive
But hidden and it sounded like applause
That would never end, and when you saw
It every time was like the first time,

Quick sun darting on white stones,
Gems flaring in the pulse and tangle
Of the water, colors in the angle
Of the clerestory light that shone

And slanted through a nave of gold
Leaves, poplar and gum turning early
In the high summer, and you hurried
To the river and entered the cold

Current and felt the water surge and rise
Around you like a garment that fit,
And when the light faded to admit
At last the black and clamorous night

The river sang above the cricket din
Like your grandfather's high tenor,
Secure in the quivering dark, forever
Measured and attuned, and when

Tony Owens

You woke into the bird-loud birth
Of an unstained day, you saw light shiver
On new water while the river
Hymned the doomed profusion of the earth.

....

Light sparking on an oil sheen recalls
You. The wide water licks at debris
Clinging to ruined banks. You cannot see
Through rising mist where the shrill cicada calls.

The last sun falls and flashes at the sky's
Red rim. Bullfrog tremors swell into the night.
You turn and stumble as the light dies
Away; you walk where the lost river lies.

Was a River

The whole of nature is surrounded by the divine. Aristotle

The river was a primitive hymn
lined out in a chapel, the call
and the unkempt response.

The river was a Dorian chant,
The quick rise and minor fall,
the bittersweet melisma.

The river was a chalice of red water
spilled and prodigal after rain.

The river was a reliquary of light
Leaking through cracked water.

The river was a thurible of mist
disappearing in a storm-seared sky.

Wait

Time like an ever-rolling stream bears all its sons away. Isaac Watts

You have only to wait,
For time defies all finalities
And time will arrive, however late,
And call the buried river to rise.

For water has hewn granite to sand,
And rapids have etched stone.
Mountains have trembled and leapt
And the highest hills made low.

You have only to wait,
For the earth to shudder and stretch,
For the rain to arrive and remain,
For the forgotten current to crest.

You have only to wait,
For the river lies dormant but alive,
And time will call the river to rise.

The Song

In memory of Lillian Parsons Owens (1929 – 2013)
Behold, I will extend peace to her like a river. Isaiah 66:12

Generations of the blood, singing the old songs
Of grace and glory, songs consonant with the kin
Around the old upright, most of them gone
Into time's slow decline, but in memory's pristine
Revival luminous and keen, taking the part
Bequeathed with the first beating of the heart.

Someone in that radiant room called *Peace Like a River*,
And the altos took up the melody and began to sing,
The basses rolling underneath like dark water, tenors
High and timely on the downbeat, sopranos flowing
Like rapids over water-smooth stones, the voices ever
Twining and abiding like rain disappearing in a river.

For the song had taken the singers and made them one,
And the singers became the song that was sung.

Postscript

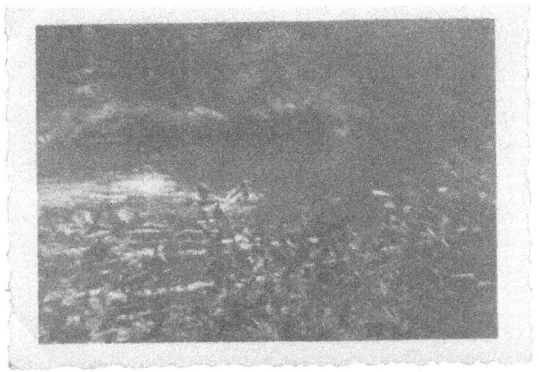

Who can faint, when such a river,
ever will their thirst assuage.
John Newton

Acknowledgments

These poems reflect my belief that creation is a mirror, however dimmed and diminished by our lack of perception, of the attributes of the Creator. So I am profoundly grateful that I knew the Keowee River while it was wild and free and I will always cherish the time spent with grandparents, parents, siblings, uncles, aunts, and cousins in that radiant river valley.

I am grateful to the professionals at Redhawk Publications for their kind assistance in bringing this volume to publication.

I am grateful to biographer *nonpareil* Joseph Pearce for reading these poems with understanding and sensitivity and pronouncing them worthy.

And I am especially grateful to Ron Rash, both for the many splendid poems, stories, and novels he has crafted over the years and for his generous encouragement and support. Thank you, Ron.

About the Author

Tony Owens was born in Pickens County, South Carolina and spent many enjoyable hours at his grandfather's cabin on the Keowee River. He holds graduate degrees in Writing and American Literature. He has taught at the college level and worked as a training consultant/ instructional developer for major corporations. He currently teaches courses on traditional music and the arts at OLLI/Furman University in Greenville, South Carolina.

www.ingramcontent.com/pod-product-compliance
Lightning Source LLC
Chambersburg PA
CBHW031219090426
42736CB00009B/991